SUMMARY OF DEMYSTIFYING THE PROPHETIC

Understanding The Voice Of God For The Coming Days Of Fire

JOSEPH Z

Copyright 2024–Harrison House

All rights reserved. This book is protected by the copyright laws of the United States of America. This book may not be copied or reprinted for commercial gain or profit. The use of short quotations or occasional page copying for personal or group study is permitted and encouraged. Permission will be granted upon request. Unless otherwise indicated, all scripture quotations are taken from the *King James Version* of the Bible. Used by permission. All rights reserved.

All emphasis within Scripture quotations is the author's own. Please note that Harrison House's publishing style capitalizes certain pronouns in Scripture that refer to the Father, Son, and Holy Spirit, and may differ from some publishers' styles. Take note that the name satan and related names are not capitalized. We choose not to acknowledge him, even to the point of violating grammatical rules.

Harrison House P.O. Box 310, Shippensburg, PA 17257-0310

This book and all other Harrison House's books are available at Christian bookstores and distributors worldwide.

For Worldwide Distribution.

Reach us on the Internet: www.harrisonhouse.com.

ISBN 13 TP: 9781667507651

ISBN 13 eBook: 9781667507354

CONTENTS

Introduction	v
1. The Voice of God from the Mountain	1
2. Conversations in Heaven	5
3. Multidimensional God	9
4. The Prophetic Spectrum	13
5. Prophetic DNA—Witchcraft or Legitimate?	17
6. Encounters with the Spirit	21
7. The Map and The Territory	24
8. A Better Hermeneutic	28
9. Two Prophecies, One King	32
10. Sensus Plenior	36
11. The Mystery of Appointed Times and People	40
12. Gatekeepers to the Spirit Realm	44
13. Mysteries and Strange Happenings	48
14. Angels of Light and Doctrines of Demons	52
15. Harnessing the Experience	56
16. The Counterfeit Anointing	60
17. False Prophets	64
18. Encountering Prophets	67
19. Office of the Prophet	71
20. A Prophet's Reward	75
21. De-Institutionalizing a Revelation	79
About the Publisher	83

INTRODUCTION

"Demystifying the Prophetic" delves into the enigmatic and often misunderstood realm of prophetic ministry within contemporary Christianity. This book clarifies the authentic role and purpose of prophets by examining their biblical foundations and demonstrating their relevance in today's complex world. Through a blend of scriptural analysis, historical context, and personal anecdotes, the author seeks to unravel the mysteries surrounding this pivotal ministry, highlighting its crucial function in guiding, warning, and revitalizing the spiritual community.

As the world navigates increasing moral and spiritual challenges, the need for prophetic voices that can offer clarity and direction becomes more apparent. "Demystifying the Prophetic" addresses this need by presenting practical insights into how prophets operate within the church and society. The book explores the dynamics of prophetic ministry, including its challenges and triumphs, aiming to equip readers with the knowledge to discern genuine prophetic messages amidst the noise of false claims.

This summary distills the essential themes and lessons from the book, providing readers with a concise and accessible overview that empowers them to engage with prophetic ministry thoughtfully and effectively. By understanding the characteristics of true prophets and the transformative power of their messages, readers are better prepared to respond to the divine call of prophecy in their own lives and communities, fostering a deeper connection with spiritual truths and divine guidance.

CHAPTER 1

THE VOICE OF GOD FROM THE MOUNTAIN

Bible Verse

"Then the Lord called yet again, 'Samuel!' So Samuel arose and went to Eli, and said, 'Here I am, for you called me.' He answered, 'I did not call, my son; lie down again.' Now Samuel did not yet know the Lord, nor was the word of the Lord yet revealed to him." - 1 Samuel 3:4-7

Introduction

In "The Voice of God from the Mountain," the author describes their personal experiences of hearing a mysterious voice during their youth, which was later understood as divine communication. This phenomenon is paralleled with biblical narratives of God's powerful and direct communication from mountaintops, illustrating how divine messages have historically intersected with human affairs.

Word of Wisdom

"Just as God called to Moses out of the burning bush, I would learn He was calling out to me." Joseph Z

Main Theme

The chapter explores the concept of divine communication as a profound, life-altering encounter that transcends ordinary experience, linking personal anecdotes with biblical events to convey the impact and reality of God's voice in human lives.

Key Points

• The author frequently heard a voice calling them by name, initially mistaking it for their father's voice.

• These encounters are compared to biblical scenes of divine presence, such as God speaking to Moses from Mount Sinai.

• The intense experiences at Mount Sinai are described vividly, emphasizing the sensory overload of sight, sound, and spiritual presence.

• God's voice is portrayed as both a literal and metaphorical force, capable of penetrating physical and spiritual realms.

- The chapter discusses the implications of hearing God's voice, both in biblical times and in contemporary settings.

- The nature of prophecy is explored, highlighting its significance and necessity in understanding divine will.

Key Themes

- **Divine Encounters as Transformative Events:** The author draws parallels between their experiences and Moses' encounters with God, suggesting that hearing God's voice is a transformative event that provides direction and purpose.
- **The Physicality of Divine Presence:** Descriptions of Mount Sinai enveloped in smoke and fire illustrate the tangible aspects of God's presence, reinforcing the power and majesty of divine encounters as witnessed by entire communities.
- **Prophecy and Perception:** The chapter delves into the role of prophecy in religious and personal contexts, arguing that understanding and responding to prophecy is crucial for spiritual growth and awareness.
- **The Role of Mediators in Divine Communication:** The necessity of mediators, like Moses in the Old Testament and Jesus as the ultimate mediator, is emphasized, illustrating their roles in facilitating a safe and meaningful connection between humanity and the divine.

- **Modern Relevance of Ancient Voices:** The author connects ancient divine communications with contemporary spiritual experiences, suggesting that the voice of God is timeless and continues to be relevant in guiding the faithful today.

Conclusion

"The Voice of God from the Mountain" serves as a compelling narrative that blends personal experience with theological insight, offering readers a nuanced understanding of how divine communication shapes faith and action. It emphasizes the continuity of God's engagement with the world and invites readers to listen more closely to the spiritual dimensions of their lives.

CHAPTER 2

CONVERSATIONS IN HEAVEN

Bible Verse

"For now we see through a glass, darkly; but then face to face: now I know in part; but then shall I know even as also I am known." - 1 Corinthians 13:12 KJV

Introduction

In "Conversations in Heaven," the narrative shifts to Heather's transformative encounter in heaven following a severe accident. This chapter not only recounts a personal spiritual experience but also delves into the broader themes of divine communication and the nature of language both before and after the fall of humanity.

Word of Wisdom

"When the Lord spoke, she knew it; when Heather spoke, the Lord knew it."
Joseph Z

Main Theme

The chapter examines the profound and personal ways in which God communicates with individuals, contrasting earthly and heavenly forms of communication and exploring the implications of these interactions for understanding divine will and purpose.

Key Points

- Heather experienced a near-death encounter that led to a profound spiritual experience in heaven.
- Communication in heaven was direct and heart-to-heart, without the need for spoken words.
- This form of communication echoes the primordial language believed to have existed in the Garden of Eden.
- Heather's experience offers insights into the nature of spiritual communication and the potential of human understanding.
- The chapter suggests that spiritual communication transcends conventional language, offering a purer, more direct form of interaction.
- Modern spiritual practices like speaking in tongues are discussed as ways to tap into this more direct line of communication with the divine.

Key Themes

- **Transformation Through Divine Encounter:** Heather's journey to heaven and her conversation with God transform her understanding of life and spirituality. This personal transformation highlights the impact that direct communication with God can have on an individual.
- **Heavenly vs. Earthly Communication:** The chapter contrasts the vivid, direct communication experienced in heaven with the more obscure and indirect methods of communication on Earth. This contrast is used to underline the limitations of earthly language and the clarity of spiritual communication.
- **Language and the Fall of Man:** The narrative explores how the fall of man altered the nature of communication from a direct and clear exchange to a more complex and less intuitive form of interaction using spoken languages.
- **The Role of Language in Spiritual Practice:** The chapter discusses the role of speaking in tongues as a spiritual practice that mirrors the direct communication of heavenly language, suggesting that such practices can enhance one's spiritual sensitivity and connection to God.
- **Prophecy and Perception in Communication:** The ability to communicate directly with God is linked to the biblical and spiritual concept of

prophecy, which involves not only predicting the future but also understanding and conveying God's will in the present.

Conclusion

"Conversations in Heaven" offers a compelling exploration of the nature of divine communication, using Heather's heavenly experience as a case study to explore broader spiritual concepts. It challenges readers to consider the depths of their own spiritual communications and to seek a clearer, more direct relationship with the divine through practices that echo the pure, heart-to-heart communication described in the chapter.

CHAPTER 3

MULTIDIMENSIONAL GOD

Bible Verse

"Then I will take away My hand, and you shall see My back; but My face shall not be seen." - Exodus 33:23

Introduction

"Multidimensional God" delves into the profound concept that God operates beyond the usual constraints of time and space, as illustrated through biblical narratives and prophetic insights. This chapter explores how divine revelations and the nature of God's existence challenge our understanding of reality, offering a glimpse into the infinite scope of God's perspective.

Word of Wisdom

"God doesn't see a parade moment by moment as it travels by. He sees things

from above, seeing the entire parade from the beginning to the end." Joseph Z

Main Theme

The main theme of this chapter is the exploration of God's multidimensional nature and His ability to interact with the universe beyond human comprehension of time and space, offering a unique perspective that enhances our understanding of prophecy and divine revelation.

Key Points

- God's perspective transcends the linear progression of time and space as understood by humans.
- Biblical figures like Moses, Daniel, and John received glimpses of God's multidimensional nature through visions and revelations.
- Prophecy is described as an unveiling where God communicates insights from beyond our physical realm.
- The concept of God viewing history as a compressed timeline offers a unique perspective on His eternal nature.
- The visions of Ezekiel and the descriptions of heavenly creatures suggest interactions with a reality that operates on multiple dimensions.
- Understanding God's multidimensional nature can deepen our grasp of biblical prophecy and our spiritual experiences.

Key Themes

- **The Eternal Perspective of God:** Viewing events from God's perspective is like compressing centuries into days, which emphasizes His eternal nature and the briefness of human history in comparison. This analogy helps readers grasp the vastness of God's oversight and His involvement in the flow of history.
- **Prophecy as Multidimensional Communication:** Prophecy is not just foretelling or forecasting; it is a complex interaction where God allows glimpses of His eternal perspective to intersect with our temporal existence. This interaction enhances our understanding of divine will and the spiritual realm.
- **Biblical Accounts of Divine Encounters:** Figures like Ezekiel and John experienced visions that are difficult to describe in human language, suggesting that these prophets were exposed to aspects of God's reality that go beyond ordinary human experiences, possibly even touching on other dimensions.
- **Concept of Time and Space in Scripture:** The Bible hints at a universe much more complex than our current understanding, with space being described in terms that suggest flexibility, such as being torn, worn out, or rolled up. These descriptions imply additional dimensions and a space-time continuum that God can manipulate.

- **Implications for Human Understanding of God:** Recognizing that God operates on a multidimensional level challenges and expands our theological and existential perceptions. It suggests that our relationship with God and our understanding of His workings can also transcend traditional religious confines.

Conclusion

For the church to function at its highest potential, it must embrace the diversity and strength of the fivefold ministry. The prophetic voice, alongside the apostolic, evangelistic, pastoral, and teaching roles, is crucial for guiding the church through current and future challenges, ensuring that it remains grounded in Christ's example and directive.

CHAPTER 4

THE PROPHETIC SPECTRUM

Bible Verse

"Formerly in Israel, when a man went to inquire of God, he spoke thus: 'Come, let us go to the seer'; for he who is now called a prophet was formerly called a seer." - 1 Samuel 9:9

Introduction

In "The Prophetic Spectrum," the chapter explores the various manifestations of prophecy within the Christian faith, distinguishing between the spiritual gift of prophecy and the office of the prophet. It emphasizes the accessibility of prophetic gifts to all believers and explains the responsibilities and roles of those called to the prophetic office.

Word of Wisdom

"Yes, responsibility is the difference

between the gift of prophecy and the office of the prophet." Joseph Z

Main Theme

The chapter details the four types of prophetic operations within the church, emphasizing the broad accessibility of these gifts to all believers while outlining specific roles for those called to the prophetic ministry.

Key Points

- Prophecy is not limited to prophets but is a gift that can manifest in any believer.
- The distinction between the gift of prophecy and the office of the prophet is primarily about responsibility and jurisdiction.
- Prophets have a specific role within the body of Christ, which includes jurisdiction over certain groups.
- The four types of prophecy include: Roeh (Visionary Seer), Nabi (Proclaiming Prophet), Chazah (Gazing Prophet), and Chozeh (Beholder).
- Prophecy functions to edify, exhort, and comfort, guiding both the church and individuals in spiritual growth and understanding.

Key Themes

- **Accessibility of Prophetic Gifts:** Every believer has the potential to operate in prophetic gifts, such as the word of knowledge, by desiring and developing these gifts through spiritual practice. This accessibility empowers believers to contribute actively to the spiritual health and dynamism of their communities.
- **Responsibilities of the Prophetic Office:** Those who hold the prophetic office carry a greater responsibility, not just in their prophetic utterances but in leading and providing accountability within the church. Their role is crucial in guiding the church through their deeper connection to God's will.
- **Differentiation in Prophetic Roles:** The four types of prophecy outline specific ways prophets can receive and convey God's messages. This differentiation helps in understanding how prophecy operates within the church, ensuring that these gifts are used effectively to build up the church.
- **Prophecy as a Spiritual Tool:** Prophecy is a tool for spiritual growth and edification. It helps the church to navigate spiritual realities and challenges, providing guidance and revelation that are instrumental in the church's mission.
- **Prophetic Authority and Jurisdiction:** A prophet's authority is not universal but is specific to certain groups or areas as designated by God. This targeted jurisdiction ensures that prophetic voices

are relevant and appropriately directed within the body of Christ.

Conclusion

"The Prophetic Spectrum" offers a comprehensive overview of how prophecy functions within the Christian community, highlighting the accessibility of prophetic gifts to all believers and the unique responsibilities of those called to the prophetic office. It encourages believers to seek and nurture these gifts, promoting a more spiritually aware and responsive church environment.

CHAPTER 5

PROPHETIC DNA— WITCHCRAFT OR LEGITIMATE?

Bible Verse
"Then the Lord took me as I followed the flock, and the Lord said to me, 'Go, prophesy to My people Israel.'" - Amos 7:14-15

Introduction

"Prophetic DNA—Witchcraft or Legitimate?" explores whether prophetic gifts can be inherited through family lines or if they are uniquely bestowed by God to individuals regardless of lineage. This chapter examines historical and biblical evidence of prophetic abilities manifesting across generations within families, and discusses the implications of such inheritances.

Word of Wisdom

"I am inclined to believe gifts can be something certain people are simply born with." Joseph Z

Main Theme

The main theme of this chapter is the exploration of the idea that prophetic abilities might be part of one's genetic makeup or family heritage, questioning whether these gifts are passed down through generations or if they are solely divinely appointed.

Key Points

- Historical instances in the author's family suggest a lineage of prophetic abilities.
- The Bible presents cases where spiritual gifts, including prophecy, seem to run in families.
- The distinction between true prophetic gifts and witchcraft or psychic abilities is crucial.
- The nature of prophetic gifts raises questions about their origin—whether divine or inherited.
- Misunderstandings and misrepresentations of prophetic gifts can lead to misuse or rejection in religious communities.

Key Themes

- **Hereditary vs. Divine Origin of Gifts:** The chapter debates whether prophetic gifts are inherited or divinely given. The biblical characters like Timothy and Philip's daughters, who exhibited faith and prophetic gifts possibly passed down from their ancestors, are examined to support the notion of hereditary spiritual gifts.

- **Responsibility and Misunderstanding of Prophetic Gifts:** There is a significant focus on the responsibility that comes with prophetic gifts and the potential for misunderstanding within the church community. Proper education and guidance are essential for those who exhibit these gifts to ensure they are used correctly and effectively.
- **Spiritual vs. Psychic Abilities:** Distinguishing between true spiritual prophecy and psychic abilities influenced by other spirits is vital. The chapter discusses how psychic phenomena often mimic prophetic gifts but originate from a non-divine source, leading to deception.
- **Role of the Church in Guiding Prophetic Gifts:** The church's role is critical in nurturing and correctly channeling prophetic gifts. Mismanagement or rejection of these gifts can lead to alienation and misuse, while proper stewardship can enhance the church's spiritual life.
- **Impact of Family Beliefs on Spiritual Development:** The beliefs and spiritual practices of one's family can significantly influence an individual's spiritual development and manifestation of gifts. The nurturing environment can either support or suppress the development of prophetic abilities.

Conclusion

"Prophetic DNA—Witchcraft or Legitimate?" encourages a thoughtful exploration of the origins and management of prophetic gifts within the Christian community. By examining scriptural examples and personal anecdotes, the chapter highlights the potential for these gifts to be inherited and the importance of discerning their true nature and origin. It calls for careful stewardship and guidance of prophetic gifts to ensure they serve the church's mission and God's purposes, avoiding the pitfalls of deception and misuse.

CHAPTER 6

ENCOUNTERS WITH THE SPIRIT

Bible Verse
"Come up here, and I will show you things which must take place after this." —Revelation 4:1

Introduction

The chapter discusses the significant spiritual encounters that can mark the life of someone attuned to the prophetic, emphasizing the importance of aligning these experiences with the Word of God to avoid deception and to fulfill one's divine purpose.

Word of Wisdom

"Without the placement of the written Word of God firmly in their lives, experiences can pull called people away from their highest purpose." Joseph Z

Main Theme

The journey of a prophetic person is filled with supernatural encounters that must be grounded in the scripture to ensure they contribute positively to their divine calling and spiritual growth.

Key Points

- Prophetic individuals often attract supernatural encounters.
- The Word of God is essential for interpreting and validating these spiritual experiences.
- A personal account of encountering God's voice at a lake illustrates the profound personal revelations that can occur.
- Encounters can range from awe-inspiring to deeply unsettling, involving elements of spiritual warfare.
- True prophetic encounters will align with the truth of the Bible and lead to peace and obedience.

Key Themes

- **Validation of Prophetic Encounters through Scripture:** The experiences of prophetic individuals, while unique and personal, must always be tested against the truth of Scripture to prevent deception and to ensure they are from God.
- **Impact of Prophetic Encounters on Personal Faith:** Genuine encounters

with the Holy Spirit enhance understanding of the Bible, deepen one's faith, and provide clear direction in life, as seen through the transformative experiences shared from the author's life.
- **Role of the Prophetic in Spiritual Warfare:** Prophetic gifts can lead to direct confrontations with spiritual darkness, necessitating a deep reliance on scriptural authority and the power of Jesus' name to overcome adversarial forces.
- **Supernatural Encounters as a Confirmation of Calling:** Encounters that are genuinely from God serve to confirm and strengthen one's calling, equipping the individual with courage, clarity, and conviction to pursue their God-given purpose.
- **The Need for Discernment in Prophetic Experiences:** It's crucial for those with prophetic gifts to develop discernment, learning to distinguish between God's voice and other spiritual influences, and to apply biblical wisdom in responding to supernatural experiences.

Conclusion

This chapter illustrates that while prophetic individuals may experience a range of supernatural events, grounding these experiences in Scripture is crucial. It ensures they serve God's purposes and lead to growth rather than confusion or fear. Prophetic encounters, when aligned with God's Word, affirm one's calling and equip them to face spiritual challenges with authority and grace.

CHAPTER 7

THE MAP AND THE TERRITORY

Bible Verse

"For we know in part and we prophesy in part." —1 Corinthians 13:9

Introduction

This chapter delves into the nuances of prophetic understanding and interpretation, drawing a parallel between the imperfections of maps in representing territories and the limitations of prophetic visions in representing divine truths. It emphasizes the need for a grounded interpretation of these spiritual experiences.

Word of Wisdom

"Remember, the map is not the territory—the map is the map." Joseph Z

SUMMARY OF DEMYSTIFYING THE PROPHETIC

Main Theme

The chapter explores the concept that prophetic visions and insights, like maps, are merely representations and not the fullness of reality itself, stressing the importance of aligning these insights with the solid foundation of Scripture.

Key Points

• Prophetic visions are imperfect representations of divine truth, similar to how maps are reductions of the territory they represent.

Emotional, environmental, and cultural backgrounds influence individual interpretations of prophetic experiences.

It's essential to ground the interpretation of prophetic experiences in Scripture and established spiritual leadership.

A heuristic approach—using practical but imperfect methods—applies to navigating prophetic insights.

The relationship between God and believers involves a partnership where divine guidance is integrated with personal discernment.

Key Themes

- **Imperfect Representations:** Just as maps cannot fully encapsulate the territory, prophetic visions cannot fully capture the entirety of God's plans or truths. These representations require careful

interpretation and a reliance on scriptural truths to guide understanding and application.
- **Influence of Personal Background:** Individuals interpret prophetic experiences through the lens of their personal histories, emotions, and cultural backgrounds. This subjectivity underscores the need for a strong scriptural base to interpret and apply prophetic insights correctly.
- **Navigational Tools in Spirituality:** The chapter likens the use of a sensory compass in navigating prophetic experiences to using a physical compass for navigation. Both require understanding, calibration, and occasionally, correction based on a fixed point of reference—the Word of God for the former.
- **Role of Heuristic Approaches in Prophecy:** Employing heuristic methods in interpreting prophecy involves using educated guesses and intuitive judgments, which are beneficial but must be balanced with disciplined spiritual practices and scriptural alignment.
- **Partnership with the Divine:** The dynamic of prophecy involves a cooperative relationship between the divine and human, where God entrusts believers with insights that are partial and require active engagement and discernment to be fully understood and rightly applied.

Conclusion

The chapter emphasizes that while prophetic insights are valuable, they are inherently partial and imperfect, much like a map's relation to its territory. Believers are encouraged to critically and prayerfully engage with these insights, using Scripture as their ultimate guide and maintaining a humble, teachable spirit to navigate the complex terrain of spiritual experiences effectively. This approach ensures that prophetic gifts are exercised responsibly and constructively, contributing to the believer's spiritual growth and the edification of the church.

CHAPTER 8

A BETTER HERMENEUTIC

Bible Verse

"So that you may learn from us the meaning of the saying, 'Do not go beyond what is written.' Then you will not be puffed up in being a follower of one of us over against the other." —1 Corinthians 4:6 NIV

Introduction

This chapter explores the importance of a balanced approach to prophetic messages, emphasizing the necessity of proper revelation, interpretation, and application to prevent misunderstandings and misrepresentations of divine messages.

Word of Wisdom

"Prophecy is not always released in a laboratory environment with perfect conditions and accuracy." Joseph Z

SUMMARY OF DEMYSTIFYING THE PROPHETIC

Main Theme

The chapter discusses the intricacies of handling prophetic revelations responsibly, focusing on the correct interpretation and practical application of these divine insights to ensure they are beneficial and correctly understood.

Key Points

• Prophetic messages can be powerful and impactful, but they may not always manifest as predicted.

Misinterpretations or over-speculations of prophetic words can lead to confusion and disillusionment.

The true intent of a prophetic message can be lost in translation, akin to the game of telephone.

Personal biases and doctrinal views can skew the interpretation of prophetic revelations.

A responsible approach to prophecy involves discerning the heart of the message rather than fixating on specific details.

Proper application of prophetic insights involves patience, waiting for divine confirmation before acting.

Key Themes

- **Importance of Contextual Interpretation:** A prophetic message needs to be understood in its correct context. Misinterpretation can lead to actions that are out of alignment with God's timing or intent, as illustrated by anecdotal mistakes where individuals acted prematurely or misguidedly based on misunderstood prophecies.

- **Role of Personal Bias in Prophecy:** Personal biases and the doctrinal lenses through which individuals view prophecies can significantly influence how they interpret these divine messages. Recognizing and mitigating these biases is crucial for a clear understanding of what the Spirit is truly communicating.
- **Necessity of Discernment in Application:** Discerning the heart of a prophetic word is more crucial than getting caught up in the specifics. This approach helps in extracting the core message that God intends to convey, which is essential for the right application in one's life.
- **Dangers of Over-Speculation:** Speculating beyond the clear meaning of a prophetic word can introduce confusion and lead to misguided actions. Staying true to the revealed word and seeking further clarity through prayer and scripture study is advised to avoid these pitfalls.
- **Proper Timing in Prophetic Fulfillment:** Understanding the correct timing for the fulfillment of prophetic words is as important as the prophecy itself. Acting without confirming the timing can lead to unnecessary hardships or failures, underscoring the need for patience and alignment with God's schedule.

Conclusion

A balanced hermeneutic approach to handling prophecy is essential for ensuring that the divine messages are accurately understood and beneficially applied. This chapter encourages readers to engage with prophetic revelations with a heart of wisdom, discernment, and faithfulness to scriptural truths, ensuring that their actions align with God's perfect timing and will.

CHAPTER 9

TWO PROPHECIES, ONE KING

Bible Verse

"But the natural man does not receive the things of the Spirit of God, for they are foolishness to him; nor can he know them, because they are spiritually discerned." —1 Corinthians 2:14

Introduction

This chapter delves into the complexities of prophetic messages, particularly when seemingly contradictory prophecies are given about the same subject. Through the biblical example of King Zedekiah, we explore how multiple prophetic perspectives can coexist and ultimately align with God's plan.

Word of Wisdom

"Both prophecies were fulfilled, and the enigma of Ezekiel explained when Zedekiah was brought to Nebuchadnezzar

at Riblah, where he had his eyes put out and was then carried to Babylon, and there died." Joseph Z

Main Theme:

The main theme addresses the reconciliation of contradictory prophecies through the story of King Zedekiah, as prophesied by Ezekiel and Jeremiah, demonstrating that differing prophetic messages can both be true from different perspectives.

Key Points

• Contradictory prophecies can coexist and both be true when viewed from the correct spiritual and scriptural perspective.

•Prophets Ezekiel and Jeremiah both gave true prophecies about King Zedekiah that seemed contradictory but were actually complementary.

• Historical and biblical context is crucial in understanding and reconciling prophetic messages.

• Prophetic messages must be discerned and interpreted with patience and a deep reliance on spiritual understanding.

• The resolution of the prophecies concerning Zedekiah illustrates how seemingly contradictory messages can form a complete and harmonious narrative when fully understood.

Key Themes

- **Harmonizing Contradictory Prophecies:** The prophecies concerning King Zedekiah by Ezekiel and Jeremiah seemed to conflict, with one saying he would not see Babylon and the other saying he would meet the Babylonian king. Both were fulfilled when Zedekiah met the king, who then blinded him, fulfilling both prophecies in a harmonious and unexpected way.
- **Importance of Spiritual Discernment:** Spiritual discernment is necessary to understand the depth and multifaceted nature of prophetic words. This discernment allows believers to see beyond the surface and grasp the spiritual truths embedded in prophecy.
- **The Role of Historical Context in Prophecy:** Understanding the historical context of prophetic messages is crucial. For example, knowing the historical outcomes and events surrounding Zedekiah's reign helps clarify how both Ezekiel's and Jeremiah's prophecies were accurate.
- **Patience and Faith in Prophecy Interpretation:** Patience is vital when dealing with prophecies. Believers are encouraged to wait faithfully for God's timing, which ensures the full and true meaning of prophetic words are realized.
- **Comprehensive Understanding of Prophecy:** It's important to approach prophecy with a comprehensive view,

considering all aspects and potential meanings, rather than hastily drawing conclusions from a single perspective.

Conclusion

This chapter teaches that multiple prophetic voices regarding the same event or person can appear contradictory but actually offer a fuller picture of God's plan when viewed together. By examining the biblical narrative of King Zedekiah through the prophecies of Ezekiel and Jeremiah, we learn the value of patience, spiritual discernment, and a holistic approach to understanding prophecy. This ensures that believers maintain faith in the divine orchestration of events as revealed through prophetic ministry.

CHAPTER 10

SENSUS PLENIOR

Bible Verse

"That which has been is what will be, that which is done is what will be done, and there is nothing new under the sun. Is there anything of which it may be said, 'See, this is new'? It has already been in ancient times before us." —Ecclesiastes 1:9-10

Introduction

This chapter explores the concept of *Sensus Plenior*, or "deeper, fuller meaning," which suggests that scriptural texts often contain layers of meaning that transcend their immediate context. This concept is particularly significant in understanding prophecy and its fulfillment across different times and situations.

Word of Wisdom

"Learn from us not to think beyond what is written, that none of you may be

puffed up on behalf of one against the other." —1 Corinthians 4:6

Main Theme

The main theme of this chapter is the exploration of the *Sensus Plenior* approach to biblical interpretation, which emphasizes the discovery of deeper meanings embedded within scriptures that are revealed over time and through fulfillment of prophecy.

Key Points

• *Sensus Plenior* refers to a deeper, more comprehensive understanding of biblical texts.

• Prophecies often serve as patterns that can reoccur or be fulfilled in various forms across different epochs.

• Traditional Western interpretations of prophecy focus on prediction and fulfillment, whereas Eastern perspectives value the recognition of recurring patterns.

• The Passover is a prime example of a prophetic pattern, with its fulfillment seen in the sacrifice of Jesus Christ.

• Scripture should be approached with humility, always aligning interpretations with the broader teachings of the Bible.

Key Themes

- **Prophecy as Pattern:** Prophecy in the Bible often serves as a template that is fulfilled multiple times in different contexts, each fulfillment adding depth and breadth to the original prophecy. This patterned approach helps believers understand complex prophecies that have both immediate and future implications.
- **Deeper Meanings in Scripture:** *Sensus Plenior* invites believers to seek the fuller meanings of biblical texts, which may not be immediately apparent. This requires a disciplined approach to scriptural study, ensuring interpretations are grounded in a comprehensive understanding of the Bible.
- **Messianic Prophecies and the Feasts:** The biblical feasts, particularly Passover, provide a framework for understanding the work of Jesus as a fulfillment of Old Testament prophecy. This illustrates how New Testament events are deeply interconnected with Old Testament practices and predictions.
- **Cautions Against Misinterpretation:** While *Sensus Plenior* provides a rich field for discovering the multifaceted nature of God's word, it also poses risks of overinterpretation. Believers are cautioned to adhere strictly to what is written and avoid speculating beyond the scriptures.
- **Application of Prophecy in Modern Times:** Understanding prophetic patterns and their fulfillments can offer powerful insights for living a faithful Christian life

today. Recognizing these patterns encourages believers to apply biblical principles dynamically and contextually in their own lives.

Conclusion

Sensus Plenior offers a profound way to engage with the Scriptures by recognizing the layered meanings within biblical prophecy. This approach not only enriches personal faith but also enhances the collective understanding of God's plans throughout history. As believers explore these deeper meanings, they are reminded to remain humble and faithful to the scriptural text, ensuring that their interpretations align with the totality of God's revealed word.

CHAPTER 11

THE MYSTERY OF APPOINTED TIMES AND PEOPLE

Bible Verse
Revelation 12:7-11
"Then He also said to the multitudes, 'Whenever you see a cloud rising out of the west, immediately you say, 'A shower is coming'; and so it is. And when you see the south wind blow, you say, 'There will be hot weather'; and there is. Hypocrites! You can discern the face of the sky and of the earth, but how is it you do not discern this time?'" —Luke 12:54-56

Introduction

This chapter delves into the biblical understanding of time, specifically focusing on the concepts of *Chronos*, *Kairos*, and *Epoch*, to illustrate how God uses time to fulfill His purposes and the roles individuals play in these processes.

Word of Wisdom

"Of the sons of Issachar who had understanding of the times, to know what Israel ought to do." —1 Chronicles 12:32

Main Theme

The exploration of different types of biblical times—*Chronos* (chronological time), *Kairos* (opportune moments), and *Epoch* (significant periods)—and their implications for understanding God's timing and our participation in His divine plan.

Key Points

- *Chronos* represents sequential time and is the typical understanding of time as a continuous flow.

- *Kairos* is about critical or opportune moments that have prophetic significance and require discernment.

- *Epoch* refers to significant periods in history or life that are marked by notable events or transformations.

- Biblical prophecies often operate within these frameworks, showing how divine moments unfold over time.

- Discerning these times is crucial for believers to align themselves with God's will and act appropriately.

- Understanding and cooperating with God's timing can significantly impact the fulfillment of His plans.

Key Themes

- **Biblical Examples of Time:** Scriptural narratives often highlight *Chronos* and *Kairos* moments, showing how events from Jesus' life to prophetic fulfillments occur within these frameworks. Understanding these examples helps believers recognize similar patterns in contemporary times.
- **The Role of Epochs in Scripture:** Epochs represent significant periods where God moves distinctly, such as the establishment of the Church post-Christ's resurrection. Recognizing these epochs helps us understand the shifts in God's dealings with humanity.
- **Prophecy and Divine Timing:** Prophecies are not just future predictions but are tied to specific divine timings (*Kairos* moments) that believers are called to discern and participate in. This participation often requires spiritual readiness and active engagement.
- **The Importance of Discernment:** Just as the sons of Issachar understood the times, believers are called to discern not only the times but also the appropriate responses. This discernment is crucial for the church to effectively fulfill its role in God's plan.

- **Practical Implications for Believers:** The understanding of time according to biblical principles affects how believers live out their faith, make decisions, and respond to God's call. It encourages a proactive stance towards living out prophecy and divine appointments.

Conclusion

The chapter emphasizes the mystery and mastery of God over time and calls believers to a deeper understanding and engagement with these divine timings. Recognizing and responding to *Chronos*, *Kairos*, and *Epoch* moments can lead to fulfilling God's purposes individually and collectively. Believers are encouraged to seek God's will actively and align themselves with His timing, thus playing their part in the unfolding of His divine plan.

CHAPTER 12

GATEKEEPERS TO THE SPIRIT REALM

Bible Verse

"So I sought for a man among them who would make a wall, and stand in the gap before Me on behalf of the land, that I should not destroy it; but I found no one." — Ezekiel 22:30

Introduction

This chapter explores the profound role of human beings as gatekeepers who bridge the natural and spiritual realms, emphasizing the necessity of human cooperation for divine interventions and prophetic actions to manifest in the natural world.

Word of Wisdom

"Then God said, 'Let there be light'; and there was light." – Genesis 1:3

SUMMARY OF DEMYSTIFYING THE PROPHETIC

Main Theme

Human beings are designed as spiritual beings with the authority to allow or deny spiritual activities in the natural world, highlighting the critical role of faith and action in activating supernatural responses.

Key Points

• Humans are inherently spiritual beings, originally created with the capacity to interact seamlessly with both the spiritual and natural realms.

• The fall of Adam restricted human access to the spiritual realm, necessitating divine intervention for restoration.

• Human cooperation is required for the spiritual to manifest in the natural; this is evident in biblical actions such as salvation, healing, and giving.

• Authority in the natural world is linked to our physical existence; spiritual forces require human permission to operate on earth.

• Jesus Christ, by taking on human form, legally restored God's dominion on earth, demonstrating the importance of physical presence for spiritual authority.

• Our spiritual actions, like prayer and obedience, have the power to trigger divine movements and reactions.

Key Themes

- **The Dual Realms of Existence:** Humans are created to exist simultaneously in both spiritual and natural realms, but the fall primarily confined us to the natural. Restoration of spiritual connection is achieved through rebirth in Christ, re-establishing our ability to interact with the divine.
- **The Role of Human Authority:** As gatekeepers, humans have the authority to either grant or deny the spiritual realm's influence in the natural world. This authority is fundamental to how prophecy and spiritual intercessions are realized in our physical reality.
- **Faith-Action Principles:** Spiritual outcomes often depend on physical actions, such as speaking, touching, or giving. These actions, rooted in faith, can catalyze supernatural responses, demonstrating the interconnectedness of belief and manifestation.
- **The Impact of Jesus' Incarnation:** Jesus' embodiment of God in human form is the ultimate expression of spiritual authority exercised within the constraints of the natural world. His life illustrates how divine purposes are fulfilled through human willingness and obedience.
- **The Continual Relevance of Spiritual Authority:** Modern believers must understand their role as spiritual gatekeepers, using their God-given authority to influence the world for Christ.

This involves discerning spiritual realities and aligning our actions with God's will.

Conclusion

The chapter underscores the critical importance of recognizing and exercising our spiritual authority as believers. By understanding our roles as gatekeepers between the spiritual and natural realms, we are equipped to make decisions and take actions that allow God's power and purposes to manifest on earth. As we engage with the world through the lens of spiritual authority, we become active participants in God's ongoing story, shaping history according to His divine will.

CHAPTER 13

MYSTERIES AND STRANGE HAPPENINGS

Bible Verse

"But God has revealed them to us through His Spirit. For the Spirit searches all things, yes, the deep things of God." — 1 Corinthians 2:10

Introduction

This chapter delves into the complexities and nuances of supernatural encounters within a Christian context, emphasizing the need for discernment and alignment with biblical truths in understanding and interpreting these experiences.

Word of Wisdom

"Label Caging" the supernatural reduces profound spiritual experiences into simplistic, controllable terms, often lim-

iting the full understanding and appreciation of God's mysterious ways. Joseph Z

Main Theme

The central theme of this chapter is the balance between open-mindedness and discernment in the Christian approach to supernatural phenomena, stressing the importance of scripture as the ultimate standard for testing all spiritual experiences.

Key Points

• Supernatural encounters are often beyond human comprehension, requiring both faith and skepticism to navigate.

• The Bible serves as the ultimate standard against which all supernatural experiences should be measured.

• Prophecy and supernatural encounters are highly subjective, with personal interpretation playing a significant role.

• Labeling supernatural experiences can limit understanding and prevent deeper spiritual insight.

• Experiences that contradict scriptural teachings should be dismissed to maintain spiritual integrity.

Key Themes

- **Subjectivity of Spiritual Encounters:** Supernatural experiences are deeply personal and can vary widely in interpretation and significance. While personal revelation is valuable, it must always be tested against the truth of the Bible to prevent deception.
- **Dangers of "Label Caging":** Simplifying complex spiritual phenomena into easily digestible labels can confine and restrict the broader, often mysterious intentions God might have, reducing the richness of divine communication to mere clichés.
- **Navigating Unusual Phenomena:** Encounters such as visions, dreams, and spiritual visitations should be approached with a balanced mindset that neither dismisses them outright nor accepts them without critical biblical evaluation.
- **The Role of Discernment:** Christians are called to discern the origin and purpose of their supernatural experiences, relying on the Holy Spirit and scriptural guidance to validate or refute these occurrences.
- **Integration of Experience with Scripture:** All spiritual experiences must be aligned with biblical teachings; any experience that deviates from scriptural truths should be considered suspect and potentially harmful.

Conclusion

"Mysteries and Strange Happenings" encourages believers to approach supernatural phenomena with a discerning heart, anchored firmly in the teachings of scripture. By maintaining a balance between openness to the Holy Spirit's work and adherence to biblical doctrine, Christians can navigate the complexities of spiritual encounters effectively and faithfully. The chapter concludes with a call to prioritize scriptural truth over sensational experiences, ensuring that our spiritual lives are both enriched and protected by the Word of God.

CHAPTER 14

ANGELS OF LIGHT AND DOCTRINES OF DEMONS

Bible Verse

"Let no one cheat you of your reward, taking delight in false humility and worship of angels, intruding into those things which he has not seen, vainly puffed up by his fleshly mind." — Colossians 2:18

Introduction

This chapter explores the escalating interest in supernatural phenomena and the dangers of prioritizing extra-biblical experiences over scriptural truths, warning against the seductive allure of "angels of light" and demonic doctrines that can lead believers astray.

Word of Wisdom

"An encounter alone should not be the verification for any scenario when it comes to supernatural events—especially in

the arena of the prophetic as it relates to angels, heaven, and various outlandish scenarios." Joseph Z

Main Theme

The central theme focuses on the critical balance between openness to genuine spiritual experiences and the steadfast anchoring in biblical doctrine to guard against deception.

Key Points

• Supernatural encounters must be validated by Scripture to prevent deception.

• The fascination with supernatural phenomena can lead to spiritual error or even occultic practices.

• There is a real threat of deception not just from external sources but from self-deception as well.

• True spiritual experiences should direct glory to God and align with biblical truths.

• Discernment is crucial for distinguishing genuine spiritual encounters from demonic deceptions.

Key Themes

- **Danger of Extra-Biblical Encounters:** Engaging with supernatural experiences that lack biblical foundation can lead believers into deception, making them susceptible to false teachings and demonic

influences. These experiences often sensationalize spirituality without substantive doctrinal backing.
- **The Role of Discernment in Spiritual Experiences:** Believers must exercise discernment when encountering spiritual phenomena, using Scripture as the definitive guide. This involves recognizing and rejecting experiences that contradict biblical teachings or elevate sensationalism over sound doctrine.
- **Deception from False Spiritual Authorities:** The chapter warns against false prophets and teachers who masquerade as servants of righteousness but lead believers away from the truth. These individuals often exploit the fascination with the supernatural to manipulate and mislead.
- **Self-Deception and Inner Integrity:** Self-deception is highlighted as particularly dangerous because it involves believers convincing themselves of the spiritual validity of unscriptural experiences. Maintaining inner integrity requires honesty about one's spiritual experiences and alignment with the Word of God.
- **Consequences of Spiritual Deception:** The spiritual, emotional, and communal consequences of deception are profound. Believers are urged to remain vigilant and grounded in Scripture to prevent the erosion of their faith and the integrity of their witness.

Conclusion

"Angels of Light and Doctrines of Demons" underscores the necessity of grounding spiritual experiences in biblical truth to safeguard against deception. It calls for a balanced approach to spirituality that embraces genuine encounters with God while rigorously testing all experiences against Scripture. The chapter serves as a cautionary tale, reminding believers to prioritize their relationship with God and His Word above the allure of the supernatural.

CHAPTER 15

HARNESSING THE EXPERIENCE

Bible Verse

"But solid food belongs to those who are of full age, that is, those who by reason of use have their senses exercised to discern both good and evil." — Hebrews 5:14

Introduction

This chapter emphasizes the critical role of character development in managing prophetic experiences, advocating for a mature handling of spiritual gifts through grounding in Scripture and personal integrity.

Word of Wisdom

"Without character, a person is unable to harness whatever experience they might have. They will be the servant of the experience rather than the master

and one who is submitted to Jesus Christ by His Word." Joseph Z

Main Theme

The necessity of character, training, and emotional intelligence in effectively managing and utilizing prophetic gifts to ensure they align with biblical truths and genuinely serve God's purposes.

Key Points

- Character acts as a safeguard, keeping prophetic individuals grounded.

- Superstition can often be mistaken for spiritual insight in the absence of biblical grounding.

- Training and practice are essential for those with prophetic gifts to avoid harm and misuse.

- Emotional intelligence enhances the ministering capability of prophetic individuals.

- Untrained sensitivity to spiritual "traffic" can lead to emotional overwhelm and misinterpretation.

- Proper handling of prophetic gifts requires a blend of spiritual sensitivity and scriptural grounding.

Key Themes

- **The Perils of Untrained Prophetic Gifts:** Individuals who operate in the

prophetic without proper training can cause significant damage, both to themselves and others. Proper training helps prevent misuse of gifts and ensures that prophetic insights are dispensed in a way that is constructive and biblically aligned.
- **Superstition versus Spiritual Insight:** A lack of solid biblical foundation can lead individuals to interpret supernatural experiences through the lens of superstition rather than divine insight. This highlights the need for a deep engagement with Scripture to correctly understand and interpret spiritual phenomena.
- **Emotional Intelligence in Ministry:** Emotional intelligence is crucial for prophetic ministers as it helps them manage their own emotions and better understand those they are ministering to. This awareness fosters deeper connections and more effective ministry by enabling ministers to meet the real needs of individuals.
- **Managing Prophetic Sensitivity ("Traffic"):** Intense emotional and spiritual sensitivity, or "traffic," can be overwhelming without proper understanding and management. Learning to control this sensitivity prevents it from overpowering the individual's life and ministry.
- **The Importance of Character and Integrity:** Strong character and integrity are essential for anyone operating in the prophetic. These qualities ensure that

spiritual gifts are used responsibly and in a manner that glorifies God, rather than serving personal or misguided ends.

Conclusion

"Harnessing the Experience" stresses the importance of building strong character, seeking thorough training, and developing emotional intelligence to manage prophetic gifts effectively. By anchoring their experiences in Scripture, individuals can avoid the pitfalls of superstition and misuse, ensuring their ministry remains true to the teachings of Christ and serves the community faithfully. The chapter serves as a call to maturity and responsibility in the stewardship of spiritual gifts, advocating for a balanced and disciplined approach to the prophetic.

CHAPTER 16

THE COUNTERFEIT ANOINTING

Bible Verse

"But the anointing which you have received from Him abides in you, and you do not need that anyone teach you; but as the same anointing teaches you concerning all things, and is true, and is not a lie, and just as it has taught you, you will abide in Him." — 1 John 2:27

Introduction

This chapter discusses the concept of a "false anointing" that mimics the true anointing of the Holy Spirit, highlighting the risks and characteristics of such deceptions. It cautions against the allure of mystical or sensational spiritual experiences that are not grounded in biblical truth.

Word of Wisdom

"Jacob understood the value of the

blessing, and in that narrative, he was able to pull deceiving his father." Joseph Z

Main Theme

The danger of counterfeit spiritual experiences that appear genuine but lead believers away from true biblical doctrine, emphasizing the need for discernment and adherence to the teachings of Scripture.

Key Points

• A false anointing appeals to the senses and mimics true spiritual experiences but lacks their divine origin.

• Mystical Christianity often leads believers into progressive deception without a solid biblical foundation.

• The story of Jacob and Esau illustrates how blessings can be manipulated and misrepresented.

• The tale of two prophets in 1 Kings 13 serves as a warning against misleading spiritual authority.

• Strange fire represents false signs and wonders that mislead believers about the nature of God's power.

• Simon the Sorcerer's attempt to buy spiritual power underscores the danger of misunderstanding and misusing the anointing.

Key Themes

- **The Allure of Mystical Experiences:** Many believers are drawn to mystical experiences that promise direct knowledge of divine realities without the mediating influence of Scripture. This often leads to spiritual deception as individuals pursue experiences over the truth of God's Word.
- **Historical and Biblical Examples of Deception:** The chapter uses historical examples, such as the false prophets from 1 Kings and figures like Esau and Jacob, to illustrate how easily the genuine can be mimicked and the sacred can be traded for immediate gratification.
- **The Consequences of False Anointings:** Engaging with false anointings can lead to serious spiritual consequences, including lost opportunities and derailment from one's divine calling. The narrative of the old prophet misleading the young prophet in 1 Kings highlights the potentially fatal outcomes of such deception.
- **Distinguishing Between True and False Fire:** The difference between God-initiated fire and man-made strange fire is crucial. True spiritual fire results in God-honoring miracles and worship, whereas strange fire leads to confusion and idolatry.
- **The Importance of Scriptural Grounding:** The chapter emphasizes that true anointing and spiritual experiences must always align with Scripture. Believers are encouraged to test every spirit and

prophetic utterance against the Word of God to prevent deception.

Conclusion

"The Counterfeit Anointing" warns against the dangers of embracing sensational and mystical experiences that deviate from biblical teachings. It calls for a return to Scripture as the foundation of faith and spiritual practice, urging believers to cultivate discernment and a deep love for the truth to safeguard against false anointings. The chapter reinforces the need for a solid biblical foundation to correctly interpret and validate genuine spiritual experiences, ensuring they contribute to growth and alignment with God's will.

CHAPTER 17
FALSE PROPHETS

Bible Verse

"And many false prophets will appear and will deceive many people." — Matthew 24:11 NIV

Introduction

This chapter warns of the dangers posed by false prophets who operate both within and outside the Church, manipulating true spiritual teachings for personal gain and leading believers astray.

Word of Wisdom

"The best way to show that a stick is crooked is not to argue about it or to spend time denouncing it but to lay a straight stick alongside it." – D.L. Moody

Main Theme

The chapter addresses the critical issue of false prophets in the Christian community, emphasizing the importance of discernment and adherence to scriptural truth to identify and resist their influence.

Key Points

• False prophets mimic genuine prophetic voices but introduce destructive heresies.

• Their appeal often lies in their ability to perform signs and wonders that captivate the unwary.

• True discernment is rooted in a love for and understanding of biblical truth.

• False prophets exploit the gullible through emotional and spiritual manipulation.

• Scriptural knowledge and a strong spiritual foundation are essential for protecting oneself from false teachings.

Key Themes

- **The Nature of False Prophets:** False prophets are characterized by their rejection of the core truths of Christianity, instead promoting a superficial form of godliness that lacks power. Their teachings lead to confusion and spiritual destruction among believers.
- **The Appeal of False Prophets:** These deceivers are often charismatic, using signs

and supposed wonders to attract and deceive followers. Their success lies in their ability to perform convincing, though ultimately misleading, miracles and signs.
- **The Consequences of Following False Prophets:** Believers who follow false prophets risk spiritual shipwreck. The deceptive teachings of false prophets not only lead away from the truth but also endanger the souls of their followers.
- **Defensive Strategies Against False Prophets:** The faithful must cultivate a deep, personal understanding of Scripture and maintain a vibrant relationship with God. This spiritual grounding helps believers discern and reject false teachings.
- **The Responsibility of Church Leaders:** Leaders within the church must be vigilant in protecting their congregations from false prophets. This includes offering clear, scripturally sound teaching and exposing any false teachings or prophets within the community.

Conclusion

"False Prophets" serves as a stark reminder of the pervasive danger of deceit within the Christian faith. It calls for vigilance and a strong, scripturally grounded faith to identify and resist the subtle encroachments of false prophets who threaten to lead many astray. By adhering closely to the teachings of the Bible and fostering a personal relationship with Christ, believers can safeguard themselves against the wiles of deception.

CHAPTER 18

ENCOUNTERING PROPHETS

Bible Verse

"Sow for yourselves righteousness; reap in mercy; break up your fallow ground, for it is time to seek the Lord, till He comes and rains righteousness on you." — Hosea 10:12

Introduction

Reflecting on numerous life-changing encounters with prophets and the supernatural, this chapter explores the profound influence of prophetic ministry experienced from childhood through adulthood, shaping the author's spiritual journey and ministry.

Word of Wisdom

"When the Spirit of God comes on me to do something, that supernatural boldness rises." Joseph Z

Main Theme

The chapter delves into the transformative impact of prophetic encounters, demonstrating how they can guide, affirm, and energize one's spiritual life and call to ministry.

Key Points

- From an early age, the author was exposed to prophetic influences, sparking a deep interest in the spiritual realm.

- A family camp orchestrated under divine inspiration marked a pivotal turning point, intensifying the author's spiritual pursuits.

- Witnessing firsthand the power of prophecy and healing cemented the author's faith and calling.

- The chapter recounts several instances where prophetic words provided direction, comfort, and foresight into personal and ministerial developments.

- Each prophetic encounter brought a deeper understanding of God's presence and voice.

- The author emphasizes the accessibility of God's voice and the importance of openness to His guidance.

Key Themes

- **Early Fascination with Prophecy:** The author's early request to God to meet a real prophet led to various encounters that confirmed and deepened his understanding of prophecy. This curiosity was foundational in developing a spiritually attuned life dedicated to pursuing and understanding God's will.

- **Transformative Encounters with Prophets:** Meetings with prophets like Dave Duell and John Paul Jackson not only brought personal healing and spiritual empowerment but also clarified the author's life mission. These encounters are depicted as turning points that significantly shaped the author's path.
- **Impact of Prophetic Ministry on Personal Life:** Prophetic words often preluded major life decisions and events, such as marriage and ministry directions, demonstrating the personal and practical applications of prophecy. The prophetic has been a compass in the author's significant life choices.
- **Continuous Openness to Prophetic Guidance:** The narrative underscores a life pattern where prophetic encounters continually guide, challenge, and affirm the author's journey. This theme illustrates the ongoing relationship between a believer and the prophetic gifts of the Spirit.
- **Prophetic Words as Tools for Encouragement and Edification:** Each prophetic encounter provided strength and affirmation needed at critical points in the author's life, highlighting the role of prophecy in edifying and equipping believers for their spiritual and earthly assignments.

Conclusion

"Encountering Prophets" encapsulates the profound impact that prophetic encounters have had on the author's life, illustrating the power of divine communication in guiding, shaping, and confirming one's spiritual walk and ministry. The narrative encourages believers to seek and be receptive to prophetic insights, emphasizing that God is continually speaking and desiring to direct the paths of those who listen. Through vivid storytelling, the chapter invites readers to explore and embrace the prophetic for transformative spiritual experiences.

CHAPTER 19

OFFICE OF THE PROPHET

Bible Verse
"And He Himself gave some as apostles, some prophets, some evangelists, and some as pastors and teachers." — Ephesians 4:11

Introduction

This chapter discusses the role and function of the prophetic office within the church, emphasizing the need for a biblical understanding to prevent dysfunction and establish clear expectations.

Word of Wisdom

"Prophets are to linger in the presence of God. To deliver the emotion of God. Making sure to really understand God's message." Joseph Z

Main Theme

The theme centers on defining the true biblical role of a prophet, differentiating it from common misconceptions, and highlighting its critical function in the church's governance and spiritual guidance.

Key Points

• Prophets function as a governmental office within the church, operating by revelation and responsibility.

• Jesus Christ is presented as the supreme model of the prophetic office.

• Prophets are more than mere foretellers; they are responsible for guiding and edifying the church.

• The New Testament era has modified the prophetic role, emphasizing interpretation over direct translation.

• The office of a prophet involves a deep, personal connection with God, allowing them to convey His will accurately.

Key Themes

- **Prophetic Responsibility Over Gifting:** The chapter clarifies that while prophets are known for their ability to see and say, their true value lies in their responsibility to the church rather than their gifting alone. This responsibility includes edifying the body of Christ and ensuring accurate conveyance of God's messages.

- **Jesus as the Ultimate Prophet:** By examining the life and ministry of Jesus, the chapter illustrates the highest standard of the prophetic office. Jesus' approach to prophecy, which combined direct communication from God with compassion and clarity, serves as the ultimate model for prophets today.
- **Shift from Old to New Testament Prophetic Role:** The transition from Old to New Testament changed the prophetic function from being a direct spokesperson for God to being a spiritual interpreter. This shift emphasizes the need for prophets to know in part and prophesy in part, reflecting a more collaborative relationship with the Holy Spirit.
- **Prophetic Integrity and Accountability:** It's discussed how New Testament prophets are expected to operate with integrity, avoiding presumption and ensuring their prophecies align with God's word. The significant consequences of false prophecies highlight the need for accountability in the prophetic ministry.
- **Cultural and Temporal Relevance of Prophecy:** The chapter touches on how the prophetic office is not just about foreseeing the future but also about speaking to current cultural and spiritual issues within the church and society. This aspect of prophecy makes it a dynamic and vital part of church leadership.

Conclusion

"Office of the Prophet" emphasizes the profound and multifaceted role of prophets within the Christian church. It advocates for a biblically grounded understanding and respect for the prophetic office, urging the church to recognize and embrace the true scope of prophetic ministry. By aligning with the biblical model and example set by Jesus, prophets can fulfill their calling to effectively guide, warn, and uplift the church community.

CHAPTER 20

A PROPHET'S REWARD

Bible Verse

"He who receives a prophet in the name of a prophet shall receive a prophet's reward." — Matthew 10:41

Introduction

This chapter delves into the concept of the "prophet's reward," exploring how honor and receptivity towards prophets unlock divine provisions and protection. It illustrates the biblical foundation and instances where prophets played pivotal roles in providing guidance, protection, and supernatural provision.

Word of Wisdom

"A man or woman with a revelation from God is never at the mercy of a culture gone mad." Joseph Z

Main Theme

The main theme focuses on the profound impact of honoring and receiving prophets, which activates a "prophet's reward" encompassing protection, guidance, and supernatural provisions as depicted through biblical narratives.

Key Points

• Prophets play a crucial role in guiding and protecting God's people through divine revelation.

• The act of receiving a prophet in honor activates the "prophet's reward."

• Historical instances, such as Samuel's interventions, illustrate the protective power associated with prophets.

• The prophet's reward includes physical provisions and spiritual insights that guard against impending adversities.

• Sowing into a prophet's ministry with the right motives can unlock supernatural outcomes.

Key Themes

- **Prophetic Intervention in Crisis:**
  Throughout biblical history, prophets have stepped in during critical times to offer guidance and deliverance, often reversing dire situations through divine intervention. Their presence and obedience have

historically led to miraculous outcomes, which are part of the "prophet's reward."

- **The Dynamics of Honoring Prophets:** The level of honor bestowed upon prophets directly influences the magnitude of the reward received. This concept is exemplified in the story of Saul seeking Samuel, illustrating that recognizing and respecting a prophet's divine role triggers spiritual and material blessings.
- **The Spiritual Mechanism of the Prophet's Reward:** This reward is not just about receiving prophecies but involves a spiritual exchange where faithfulness towards a prophet's ministry brings about God's favor and interventions. It includes protection from enemies, as seen in Samuel's life, and provision during famine.
- **Misconceptions and Abuse of the Prophet's Role:** The chapter addresses common misunderstandings and the potential misuse of the prophet's reward, emphasizing that true prophetic gifts are not for sale and warning against the commercialization of prophetic gifts.
- **Practical Implications of the Prophet's Reward:** Engaging with the prophet's reward involves more than passive reception; it requires active participation, such as sowing into a prophet's ministry and aligning one's actions with prophetic directives, which leads to multiplied blessings and divine providence.

Conclusion

"A Prophet's Reward" underscores the powerful spiritual principle that honoring and engaging with legitimate prophets under God's directive brings about divine rewards. These rewards manifest as both spiritual and material blessings, reflecting God's active presence in the lives of those who believe and respond to His prophets. Through historical examples and scriptural backing, the chapter encourages readers to recognize and honor the prophetic office as a conduit for God's grace and power in their lives.

CHAPTER 21

DE-INSTITUTIONALIZING A REVELATION

Bible Verse
"For thus says the Lord to the men of Judah and Jerusalem: 'Break up your fallow ground, and do not sow among thorns.'" — Jeremiah 4:3

Introduction

This chapter explores the prophetic role in challenging and revitalizing stagnant religious institutions by reconnecting them with their foundational truths and divine destinies. It emphasizes the need for prophets to stir institutions towards genuine spiritual renewal and away from complacency.

Word of Wisdom

"If the cause is too small, men will fight. If the cause is big enough, men will unite." Joseph Z

Main Theme

The central theme focuses on the transformative impact of prophetic voices in institutional settings, urging a return to first principles and a rekindling of the 'first love' of spiritual fervor and authenticity.

Key Points

• Prophets are tasked with revitalizing institutions by reminding them of their foundational truths.

• Prophetic ministry often involves confronting and breaking down established norms and barriers.

• True prophetic encounters can unearth and address hidden agendas or rebellion within institutions.

• Prophets facilitate a return to foundational spiritual truths, often challenging denominational divides.

• The prophetic voice seeks to inspire unity and collective action by focusing on grand, unifying causes.

Key Themes

- **Prophetic Role in Institutional Revitalization:** Prophets are not just foretellers but active participants in challenging the status quo within religious institutions, encouraging them to break away from ineffective traditions and embrace a dynamic, Spirit-led approach to faith.

- **Confrontation with Institutional Stagnation:** The presence of a prophetic voice in institutions often acts as a catalyst for change, revealing hidden resistances and prompting either persecution of the prophet or transformation of the institution. This dynamic is crucial for the spiritual awakening and reform of the institution.
- **Breaking Up Fallow Ground:** Just as fallow ground must be broken up to become fertile again, prophetic ministries are involved in breaking up the hardened structures within religious settings, making them receptive to new growth and revival.
- **Restoring First Love through Prophetic Ministry:** The prophetic calling includes helping institutions and their leaders to rediscover and recommit to their original spiritual fervor, often lost over time due to routine and complacency.
- **Encouragement of Unity and Collective Purpose:** By addressing and challenging small-minded disputes within religious communities, prophetic voices encourage focusing on larger, unifying causes that align with God's broader mission, fostering unity and collective action.

Conclusion

"De-Institutionalizing a Revelation" highlights the crucial role of prophetic voices in challenging religious complacency and urging a return to foundational spiritual truths. It calls for a reevaluation of traditional practices that may hinder spiritual growth and advocates for a prophetic engagement that rekindles passion and unity within the Christian faith. This revitalization is seen as essential for the church to fulfill its divine mandate in the world.

Harrison House is a Spirit-filled, Word of Faith Christian publisher dedicated to spreading the message of faith, hope, and love through our wide range of inspiring publications. Committed to the messages that highlight the power of the Word and Spirit, we provide books, devotionals, and study guides that empower believers to live victorious, faith-filled lives.

Our resources are designed to help readers grow spiritually, strengthen their faith, and experience the transformative power of God's Word. Harrison House is passionate about equipping Christians with the tools they need to fulfill their divine purpose and impact the world for Christ.